MW01153548

WHAT ON EARTH?
THE ENVIRONMENT

Jonathan Litton

Pau Morgan

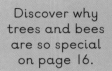

Read a poem about our Earth on page 5.

Discover why trees and bees are so special on page 16.

Contents

What is the environment?

Make your own mini greenhouse on page 24.

Is Earth in safe hands?

Find out about global warming on page 23.

Find out how to reduce your carbon footprint on page 41.

Read about the Whanganui River and the Maori on page 58.

Reduce, reuse, recycle

Local and global

Try designing your own eco-home on page 56.

Discover the truth about plastic on page 34.

Wise words

Think about the Earth and how we treat it. How does nature and the environment make you feel?

"Humankind has not woven the web of life.

We are but one thread within it.

Whatever we do to the web, we do to ourselves.

All things are bound together.

All things connect."

(Chief Seattle 1786–1866)

Deserts, mountains, deep blue seas,
Creatures, plants and noble trees.
Planet Earth is home to all;
Full of wonders, this spinning ball.

Can you write a poem about the environment?

What is the environment?

Everything on Earth is part of the environment. Living things and non-living things, natural and man-made. Air and water, plants and animals.

Air is vital for life. Keeping air free from **pollution** is a big environmental challenge.

Trees and plants provide **habitats** and food for animals. They also help to keep oxygen and **carbon dioxide** in balance.

Water naturally follows a cycle, connecting land, sea, and sky. Animals, plants, and people tap into this precious natural resource.

People have changed the face of the planet with farms, cities, and factories, but also pollution and waste.

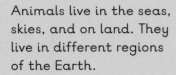

Animals live in the seas, skies, and on land. They live in different regions of the Earth.

Did you know?
The environment changes over time. Dinosaurs lived on a hotter, swampier Earth than we do. Some environmental changes are natural. Others are caused by people.

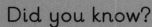

Homes and habitats

Earth has many different regions, from tropical rainforests to the icy poles. These regions house different habitats—which basically means homes for animals and plants.

Mountains are habitats too. They support different types of plants and animals than those found on lower lands.

Oceans provide many different types of habitat, from cold waters that are home to seals and penguins, to tropical oceans with coral reefs and millions of colorful fish.

Rainforests are bursting with life and full of variety. The rainwater supports lots of trees and plants. These in turn support many animals.

- Oceans
- Woodland
- Tropical Forests
- Mountains
- Grasslands
- Deserts
- Polar Regions

Animals living in the **polar regions** are adapted for the coldest habitats on the planet. Polar bears, penguins, seals, walruses, puffins and auks, all manage to survive living at the ends of the Earth.

Woodland habitats can be found in many parts of the world. There are several types, including deciduous (trees which lose their leaves in autumn) and coniferous (trees which stay green all year round).

Only well-adapted species make their homes in **desert** habitats. Camels, snakes, lizards, and fennec foxes are among animals which survive in areas with very little water.

Elephant, lions, giraffes, and zebras are among the animals found in the **grassland** or **savanna** habitats of Africa. There are also grassland regions on all continents except Antarctica.

Did you know?
As well as tropical rainforests, there are "temperate" (cool) rainforests. There's even a penguin species that lives in a rainforest in New Zealand!

Endangered species

Many species are in danger of **extinction**.
Can you match these **endangered** creatures
to their natural habitats?

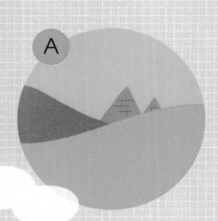

A

1

Rhinoceroses used to roam grassland regions in great numbers, but poachers have killed many for their horns.

2

Giant pandas are endangered because their bamboo forest habitat is being destroyed. Pandas get all of their nutrients from bamboo, but humans are clearing the bamboo forests for homes, roads and farms.

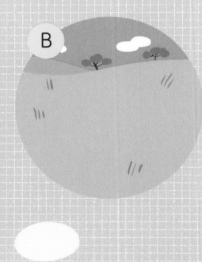

B

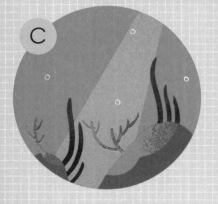

C

3

The **wild Bactrian camel** is critically endangered with only about 1,500 individuals remaining in desert and semi-desert habitats.

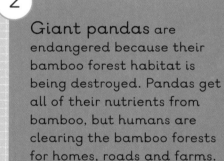

Answers: 1B, 2D, 3A, 4E, 5F, 6C

4

Polar bears are tough creatures, but they are sensitive to environmental changes. **Climate** change is causing the polar ice cap to melt, limiting the area in which polar bears can hunt.

D

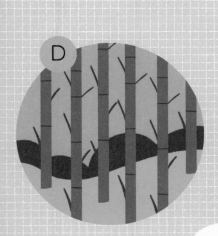

E

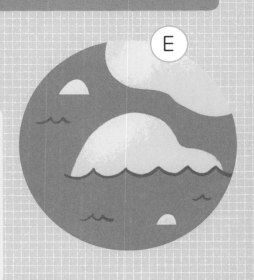

5

Orange-haired **orangutans** are seeing their tropical rainforest habitat destroyed by humans. Each year their habitat is shrinking. Unless urgent action is taken, they will become extinct.

F

6

The **blue whale** is the biggest animal in the world—it's heavier than the biggest dinosaur! It lives in an ocean environment and was almost hunted to extinction by humans. Now it is threatened by climate change and pollution.

Garden biodiversity

Even the most urban environment will be home to lots of animals— let's step outside to meet some of your wild neighbors!

Tool kit

- milk or juice carton
- scissors
- paint
- string
- sticks or twigs
- glue

Feed the birds

What to do

1 Cut a window in a washed milk or juice carton, then paint the outside of the carton and leave to dry.

2 Punch a hole in the top of the carton and push string through ready to hang the bird feeder. Then glue sticks to the carton to make a roof.

3 Punch a hole beneath the window and insert a stick for birds to land on. Add bird food inside and hang from a tree.

Tracking trays

If you're lucky, you may find animal tracks in snow, soil, or mud. But why rely on luck when you can make your own tracking tray? Fill several shallow trays with damp sand and spread these around the garden. Inspect for animal tracks in the morning. Be patient!

Visitors' book

Keep a record of animals spotted in your garden or school grounds. Take observations at different times of day. Predict what you may see and record everything in a "visitor book"!

Worm charming

Moles eat worms, so worms are afraid of moles. If you bang a rake or spade on the ground, it creates vibrations. Worms fear that these vibrations are from an attacking mole, so they'll come to the surface for safety. See how many worms you can charm in a set time. Collect them in a pot with a little soil, but make sure you return them to their habitat afterward.

Make your own microhabitats

Habitats don't have to be huge. You can create microhabitats in your back yard and study the wildlife that visits.

Mini pond

You can create a watery habitat in your yard or school quite easily. You'll need permission, help, and supervision from an adult.

Tool kit

- shovel
- plastic sheet
- bricks or tiles
- sand or gravel
- water
- sticks and leaves

What to do

1 With adult supervision, dig a hole for your pond in a suitable location.

2 Place a plastic sheet at the bottom of the hole. Use bricks or tiles to hold the sheet in place.

3 Spread sand or gravel across the sheet.

4 Add water, and see who visits.

Top tip: add water plants from a garden center around the edge of the pond to attract more visitors.

Forest floor

It takes hundreds of years for a mature forest habitat to develop. But you can create a "forest floor" environment in minutes using sticks and leaves or grasses. Insects and minibeasts will love all the holes to hide in.

What to do

1. Gather sticks and leaves that have naturally fallen from trees. If you can't find leaves, you can pick some grass instead.

2. Arrange the sticks, leaves, or grass in a pile at least 2 inches (5cm) high, and as long as you like. Make sure there are plenty of gaps.

3. Wait.

4. Watch and record visits from minibeasts.

Trees and bees

Without trees and bees, life as we know it wouldn't exist!

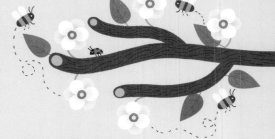

Busy bees

Without a helping buzz from bees, there wouldn't be so many trees. That's because bees carry pollen between trees. Trees need this pollen to develop seeds and new trees can grow from these seeds, thanks to the busy bees.

Super trees

Trees act as the planet's lungs. They absorb carbon dioxide and release oxygen, a gas which animals need to stay alive. They also provide habitats and food for millions of species. Helpfully, they absorb dust and pollution from the air.

Special species

Some species play special roles in keeping their habitat in balance. They are known as **keystone species.**

Elephants

Elephants trample on grasses and small trees. Without them, some parts of the African savanna would quickly become forests! The elephant is key to maintaining the ecosystem in its present form.

Beavers

Beavers use trees to create dams. The dams create lakes, making new habitats and attracting new species. Few animals shape their landscape as dramatically as the beaver.

Wolves

Without hungry wolves, there would be more grazing animals. These grazing animals would eat more of the grasses and wear away the soil, which would completely change the habitat. Wolves are therefore the guardians of places such as Yellowstone National Park in America.

Starfish

The starfish was the first keystone species identified. By keeping barnacle and mussel populations in check, it allows healthy growth of seaweed, which in turn supports healthy populations of sea urchins, sea snails, limpets, and other shellfish.

People and the planet

No species has affected the planet as much as humans. We've developed farms, towns, cities, factories, and mines, which have all changed the landscape.

Broken planet

We're hungry and thirsty for food, water, wood, metals, and minerals. We love electricity, cars, **plastics**, skyscrapers, and airplanes. We've cleared huge areas of natural habitat and created huge mountains of waste.

We can fix things

Earth is in a delicate state and we need to treat it carefully. There are steps that each and every person can do to help reverse some of the damage already done, and create a bright future for people and planet.

In safe hands?

Making a model of the Earth using tiny dots of paint can help put the planet in perspective.

Tool kit
- colored paper
- scissors
- cardboard
- blue and green paint
- 2 pencils

What to do

1 Trace your hands onto colored paper and cut them out.

2 Trace and cut out the Earth template (see p60) and glue onto cardboard. Cut the Earth out.

As you are painting your Earth, think about how big, fragile, and wonderful it is.

Is the Earth in safe hands? Think of practical steps you can take to help treat the world well (for example, **recycle**), and write these words or phrases on the hands.

3 Use the non-writing end of each pencil to paint green dots on land and blue dots on the oceans. You will need to make hundreds of little dots to cover the planet.

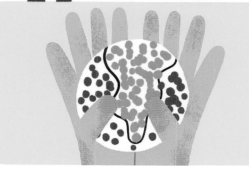

4 Use tape to glue your handprints in place, as if they are holding the Earth.

Wonderful woodland

About 30% of the Earth is covered in forests, yet they are home to about 80% of species that live on land. Millions of people live in forests too.

Deforestation

Trees are being cut down at a rapid rate. An area the size of a football field is cleared from the Amazon rainforest every minute. Why is this happening? People use the wood from trees to make buildings, furniture, paper, and other products.

Also, a lot of deforestation is caused by people using the land for villages, towns, cities, or farms. A growing population needs more and more food. Many forests are being cut down to grow crops which are fed to animals. The animals are then eaten by people.

What can we do?

Firstly, forests can be protected. This can happen by law, or by people changing their habits. Using recycled paper means new trees aren't chopped down to make paper. Secondly, new trees can be planted. **Reforestation** is happening around the world right now—millions of trees have been planted, and millions more are planned. You can plant a tree too...today!

How to plant a tree

Trees scatter many seeds, but few end up in the right conditions to grow into a new tree. Here's how to give nature a helping hand...

Tool kit

- stones
- acorn or sweet chestnut seed
- plant pot (with drainage holes)
- compost
- wire mesh

What to do

1. Add stones to the base of a plant pot and fill with compost.

2. Dig a small hole in the center about 1 inch (2.5 cm) deep. Plant the seed, cover with compost, press down, and water.

3. Cover the pot with wire mesh to prevent birds or animals eating the seed.

4. Put the pot outside in a shady spot and water about once a week.

As the young tree grows, transfer it to larger pots. When it reaches about 15 inches (40 cm), transfer it to the ground.

Did you know?

It is reported that, in 2019, 23 million people in Ethiopia planted over 200 million trees in one day! Many countries around the world have tree-planting schemes.

What is carbon dioxide?

Carbon dioxide, or CO_2, is a gas naturally found in the Earth's **atmosphere**. People breathe in oxygen from the air and breathe out carbon dioxide. Trees and plants do the opposite: they take in carbon dioxide and give out oxygen.

Unnatural emissions

The modern world is a carbon dioxide factory, and extra carbon dioxide traps heat in the planet's atmosphere, which changes the environment. There are many man-made emissions of carbon dioxide. CO_2 is released when we burn coal or drive a gasoline-fueled car.

Cleaner choices

Greener energy choices, less wasteful habits, and reforestation can all help to reduce the unnatural emissions of carbon dioxide. Today, renewable energy sources like solar, wind, and hydro power are producing more and more of our electricity.

By 2050, solar energy could be the biggest producer of energy worldwide. If we could harness the sun's power to its full extent, one hour of sunlight could generate electricity for the whole Earth for an entire year!

Around the world, hundreds of thousands of wind turbines help to harness natural energy.

Greenhouse gases and global warming

The Earth is a bit like a greenhouse. In the daytime, heat from the sun warms the planet. At night, the Earth's surface cools and heat escapes out of the atmosphere.

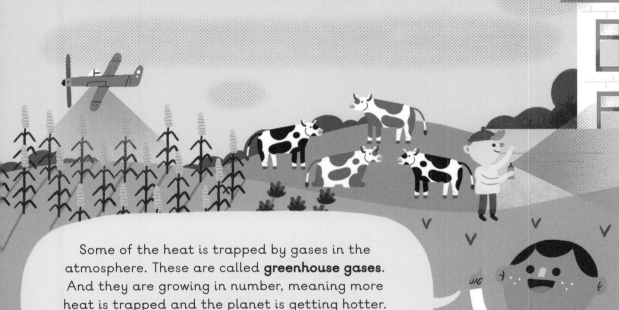

Some of the heat is trapped by gases in the atmosphere. These are called **greenhouse gases**. And they are growing in number, meaning more heat is trapped and the planet is getting hotter. This is called **global warming**. Humans are also pumping these gases into the atmosphere:

Methane
This is released through farming (cow farts, and crop-growing processes) and the burning of some materials.

Nitrous oxide
Fertilizers used in farming release this into the atmosphere. It is almost 300 times stronger than carbon dioxide as a greenhouse gas.

Fluorinated gases
These are found in many modern things like fridges and aerosols; their use has increased hugely in the past 50 years.

Make a mini greenhouse

You can actually see and experience the greenhouse effect in your back yard. Try this experiment.

Tool kit
- two large bowls
- thermometers
- electrical tape
- water
- cling film
- sunshine

What to do

1 Find a spot outside where both bowls are in equal amounts of sunlight.

2 Pour an equal amount of water into each bowl.

3 Place a thermometer into the water inside each bowl. Tape to the inside of the bowl so the temperature can be read through the bowl.

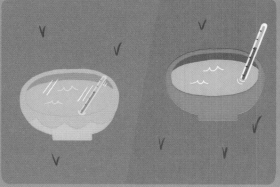

4 Cover one bowl with cling film.

5 Take the temperatures regularly and record your results. Be patient if you do not notice a change immediately, or try again on a sunnier day!

What happens?
The cling film stops some heat from escaping. It acts like a greenhouse gas. On Earth, carbon dioxide and other greenhouse gases behave like the cling film and prevent some heat from escaping the atmosphere. This means the planet stays hotter than it would have been without the greenhouse gases.

Rising sea levels

Global warming is causing polar ice caps to melt. Sea ice and land ice have different effects when they melt. Discover why in this experiment...

Tool kit
- 2 clear plastic (or glass) containers
- play dough
- water
- measuring cup
- ice cubes
- ruler
- marker

In the Arctic, there are large ice sheets floating on seawater. The ice sheets of Antarctica are mostly on land.

What to do

1 With play dough, make a continent with a flat surface, about 2 inches (5 cm) high. Add this to the center of one container. The continent should be large enough to support several ice cubes on top, but it shouldn't touch the sides of the container. This container will represent land ice.

2 Pour in water using a measuring cup until the water is about ¼ inch (5 mm) from the surface of the continent. Note how much water you added.

3 In the second container, add the same amount of water. This container will represent sea ice, as is found in the Arctic Ocean.

4 Mark the water level on the outside of the containers with a marker.

5 In the land ice container, add as many ice cubes as will fit on top of the play dough.

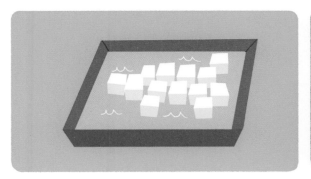

6 In the sea ice container, add the same number of ice cubes to the base of the tray.

7 Take observations every 5 minutes and mark the new water level if it has changed. Continue until the ice has melted.

What happens?

You'll notice that the sea ice water level hardly changes, but the land ice water level rises quite a lot. This is because when "land ice" melts, "new" water is flowing into the ocean from the land, and more water means a higher **sea level**. When "sea ice" melts, ice turns into water. The volume of the "new" water is about the same as the melted ice, so there is almost no change.

Did you know?

Rising sea levels mean whole communities, islands, and countries will disappear if no action is taken. The island nations of the Pacific are already being affected by this climate emergency.

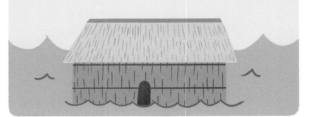

The ozone layer

Ozone is a natural gas found in the atmosphere. An **ozone layer** protects the Earth from the sun's harmful ultraviolet radiation. Keeping this natural shield in good working order will protect future generations of people, animals, and plants.

Good ozone

The ozone layer in the upper atmosphere stops harmful UV rays from reaching Earth. These rays damage plants and animals. Life on Earth would be very different if there was no upper ozone layer.

Upper ozone layer

Lower ozone layer

Bad ozone

Ozone in the lower atmosphere dirties the air and helps to cause smog, which is unhealthy to breathe.

Hole

The damage from **CFCs** and other chemicals caused a huge hole to appear in the ozone layer above Antarctica.

CFCs

CFCs are manmade chemicals which used to be found in objects like fridges and deodorants. When CFCs were released into the atmosphere, they damaged the ozone layer. These days, CFC-free alternatives are used wherever possible.

Patching things up

Reduction in the use of CFCs is allowing the ozone layer to slowly repair itself. It is predicted to be fully repaired in our lifetime.

An oily experiment

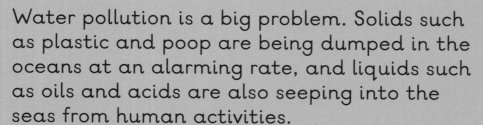

Water pollution is a big problem. Solids such as plastic and poop are being dumped in the oceans at an alarming rate, and liquids such as oils and acids are also seeping into the seas from human activities.

Oil spill

Sometimes oil tankers spill huge amounts of oil into the oceans, and it is very hard to clean up. Try it for yourself...in a bowl!

Tool kit

- large plastic container filled with water
- 1 plastic boat
- 2 plastic bottle caps
- vegetable oil
- teaspoon
- cotton wool balls
- feather

What to do

1 Add oil to the plastic bottle caps and put these "oil drums" on the boat (oil tanker). Place the oil tanker in the water.

2 Simulate a crash; spill the oil and watch it spread.

3 Now try cleaning the oil up. Is it possible to scoop it up with a teaspoon? How about absorbing it will balls of cotton wool? It's almost impossible to get rid of the oil, however hard you try.

4 Now dip the feather into the oil spill. What do you notice? Oil spills can be very harmful to wildlife, killing thousands of seabirds, fish, and other species.

What a load of rubbish!

The average person throws away over 2 pounds (almost a kilogram) of waste per day. All the people on the planet combine to throw away over 2.2 billion tons (2 billion tonnes) of solid waste a year. Much of our modern waste takes hundreds or thousands of years to **biodegrade** (break down into natural materials).

Each tonne of recycled paper can save 17 trees, 165 gallons of gasoline, 3 cubic yards of landfill space, 4,000 kilowatts of energy, and 7,000 gallons of water!

About 7.7 million tons (7 million tonnes) of food are thrown away per year, and yet many people in the world go hungry.

Problem plastic

Plastics are fantastic, right? They come in all different shapes and colors and can be used to make bottles, chairs, clothing, computer parts, and so much more. Look around you and make a list of all the plastic products you can see...

The problem with plastic

But there's a problem. Plastic doesn't biodegrade. When we throw away plastic items, they may take hundreds of years to break down. And we're using plastics at such a rate (scientists say more in the last 10 years than in the previous 100) that we're creating huge plastic rubbish mountains. What's worse, a lot of the plastic waste ends up in our oceans. At the current rate, there will be more pieces of plastic than fish in the oceans by 2050.

> Currently about half of all plastic products are designed for a single use.

Some solutions

Using plastic is a habit that we *can* break.

Plastic shopping bags can take 1,000 years to break down. By using a reusable bag from natural materials, you can save thousands of plastic bags from entering landfill. You can estimate the number by looking up the average life expectancy for your gender and nationality.

1. So if you live to 85...subtract your current age (= _____)
2. Multiply by 52 weeks a year (= _____)
3. Multiply by 5 shopping bags a week. (= _____)

The result is how many shopping bags you could save from being used in your lifetime!

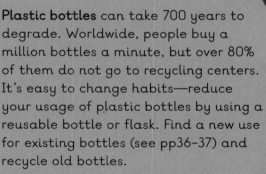

Plastic bottles can take 700 years to degrade. Worldwide, people buy a million bottles a minute, but over 80% of them do not go to recycling centers. It's easy to change habits—reduce your usage of plastic bottles by using a reusable bottle or flask. Find a new use for existing bottles (see pp36-37) and recycle old bottles.

Eating natural food like fresh fruit and vegetables is good for the environment in many ways. Processed food wastes energy and can come with a lot of packaging. Natural foods such as bananas and coconuts come in their own protective packaging...designed by nature! Eating natural food is good for the environment, and good for you, too.

A vertical garden

Want a project that reduces your **carbon footprint** and reuses and recycles plastic bottles? Then make a vertical garden, which looks fantastic and is great for the environment!

You can use an existing fence panel or a wooden pallet as the surface for your vertical garden. An adult can pick up a pallet from a garden center or recycling center (so you'd be reusing this as well as the plastic bottles). The pallet could be leaned against a wall and tied and supported to keep it upright.

You may need an adult to help with the cutting. Be careful!

Tool kit

- fence panel or wooden pallet
- scissors
- string or wire
- 6 large plastic bottles
- drill
- soil or compost
- plants

What to do

1 Cut the bottom off a plastic bottle (near where the label ends) using scissors. Ask an adult to poke two drainage holes in the bottle about 2 inches (5 cm) from the lid.

2 Fill the bottle with soil or compost and place it against the fence or palette, to make the base of the vertical garden.

3 Cut the bottoms off three more bottles. Remove the lids and fill each bottle with soil or compost. Stack them onto the bottom bottle in a tower. Tie the bottles to the fence or pallet with wire or string.

4 Take a fifth bottle and cut it in half using scissors. Take off the lid and insert the top half into the top bottle of the tower. This bottle will be a funnel.

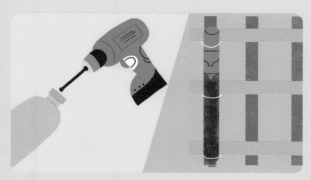

5 Cut the bottom off a sixth bottle. Ask an adult to drill a hole through the lid. This will be your water tank. Place it at the top of the tower and tie in place.

6 Ask an adult to cut windows in bottles 1, 2, 3, and 4. Add plants in these windows.

7 Then add water to bottle 6, your water tank. This water will drip through the whole tower for all the plants to enjoy. Make as many towers as you can and admire your vertical garden!

Drip, drip, drip

Water is one of the planet's most precious resources. Millions of people survive on less water per day than is wasted in one flush of a toilet! Saving water cuts down on the energy it takes to pump it to your house.

Down the drain

Using a one-liter plastic bottle, you can investigate how much water is wasted from dripping taps and leaking pipes.

1. Poke a hole in the base of the bottle with a push pin. Add some water to the bottle to see whether the hole allows water to escape, ideally one drop at a time. If the hole is too small, widen with a pencil.

2. Fill the bottle, noting its capacity. Use a stopwatch to time how long it takes for the bottle to empty.

3. Finally, you can calculate the hourly and daily wastage rate of the drip:

   Hourly wastage (liters per hour) = 60 ÷ time in minutes for the bottle to empty

   Daily wastage (liters) = hourly wastage (liters per hour) x 24

   Every drop of water saved is precious as it is available to use again!

Keep clean...and green
Showers use less water than baths. Try to take quick showers. instead of a bath.

Brushing...
Turn the tap off while you brush.

...and flushing
Water-saving devices can be added. Check with an adult.

Doing the dishes
Rinse dishes in a sink rather than using running water.

Laundry
Make sure the machine is full before washing, and only wash clothes if you really need to.

Tread carefully!

We all cause carbon dioxide to be released into the atmosphere through our activities.

Carbon footprint

Your carbon footprint is the amount of carbon dioxide you generate through your activities. The smaller your carbon footprint, the kinder you are treating the planet. For example, traveling by car or plane burns fuel which creates carbon dioxide. Even eating dinner generates carbon dioxide as food is transported from the farm to your plate.

How much carbon?

See if you can work out how much carbon dioxide each of these activities creates. Match each item to the correct weight.

Traveling 6 miles (10 km) by car

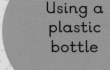

Using a plastic bottle

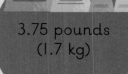

3.75 pounds (1.7 kg)

Using a computer for 2 hours

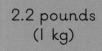

2.2 pounds (1 kg)

Traveling 6 miles (10 km) by train

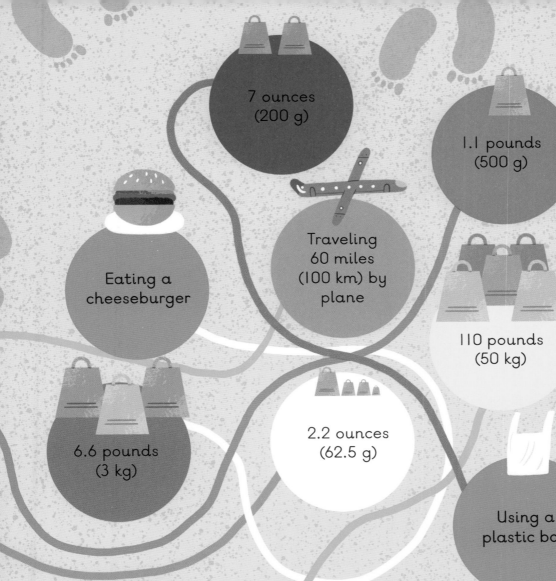

7 ounces
(200 g)

1.1 pounds
(500 g)

Eating a
cheeseburger

Traveling
60 miles
(100 km) by
plane

110 pounds
(50 kg)

6.6 pounds
(3 kg)

2.2 ounces
(62.5 g)

Using a
plastic bag

What steps can you take to reduce your carbon footprint?

- Walking and cycling when possible.
- Using buses and trains instead of cars.
- Turning off lights and electronic devices when not needed.
- Reduce, reuse, recycle—any time you can.
- Eat fresh, locally grown food when possible.

Going places

In today's connected world, people travel. A lot!
Two hundred years ago, transport choices were limited
(walk; boat; horse and cart, etc.), but today there are
hundreds of different ways to get from A to B, some
of which are better for the environment than others.

Flying

Planes cause about 2% of man-made
carbon dioxide emissions. This number
doesn't seem sky high, but planes also
release huge quantities of water vapor into
the atmosphere, which forms ice clouds.
These act like greenhouse gases, trapping
heat and causing global warming.

Foot power

Walking and cycling are great for
the environment as they are almost
carbon-neutral. (Of course, electricity
is still used when making a bike, and
the same for your shoes, unless you
walk barefoot!) These activities are
great exercise for you, too.

Driving

Roads can prevent animals making their
usual migration routes. Around the
world, wildlife-friendly tunnels and
bridges have been planned and built,
such as a crossing for mountain
lions in California.

By rail

Energy-efficient trains use technology which captures and reuses energy which would have been "lost" when braking.

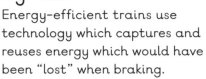
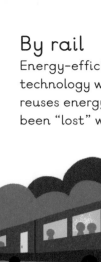

Green cars

Electric cars are replacing some fossil fuel-burning cars on the roads. They reduce carbon footprint by about 75% and are gaining in popularity. Could the fossil-fuel-powered car become extinct in 20 years?

On the seas

Cruise ships have huge carbon footprints. Passengers can be responsible for three times the emissions as they would be on land. Also, many of these "floating cities" dump waste into the oceans.

Fashion and pollution

It's not quite as bad as oil but the fashion industry is one of the largest polluters in the world. Why is it so bad, and how can it be given an environmental makeover?

Water consumption

1.5 trillion tons (1.36 trillion tonnes) of water are used by the fashion industry every year. Water is used to dye and prepare fabrics, and also to grow cotton and other plant-based fabrics.

Waste

The average family in North America throws away 66 pounds (30 kg) of clothes per year. Textile factories create huge mountains of waste. Many modern fabrics take 200 years to biodegrade.

Water pollution

Toxic chemicals are used to dye fabrics and in many countries these are dumped directly into rivers and streams from textile factories. Fertilizers used on cotton plants also cause pollution which enters our rivers and oceans.

Greenhouse gases

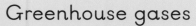

About 10% of the world's greenhouse gases come from the fashion industry. Huge amounts of energy are used to produce and transport clothes across the globe.

Deforestation

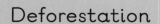

Seventy million trees are cut down every year to make clothes. Rainforests are cleared and replaced by plantations, used to make wood-based clothing materials like rayon and viscose.

Microfibers

Modern clothes are often made from microfibers—tiny artificial particles thinner than a human hair. Every time such clothes are washed, harmful microfibers enter our rivers and oceans. Microfibers are now the most common type of pollution on our coastlines. They can even be found in rainwater. Choosing clothes made from natural materials will help prevent more microfibers from entering our ecosystems.

Sustainable fashion

If we think about clothing rather than fashion then we're on the path to sustainability. Buying fewer items of clothing will help reduce waste and pollution. Buying durable clothes and recycling clothes will prevent waste too. Natural materials are better for the environment than manmade materials. Sustainability will never go out of fashion!

45

A solar oven

Rather than burning wood or charcoal to cook food outdoors, you can use solar power, which will reduce your carbon footprint. You'll also be reusing cardboard packaging, for extra environmental-friendliness. Wait for a hot, sunny day without wind for the best results.

Tool kit

- big pizza box
- pencil
- ruler
- black paper
- craft knife
- aluminum foil
- white glue
- cling film
- shipping tape or black electrical tape
- wooden skewer, stick, chopstick, or pencil
- marshmallows, graham crackers, and chocolate

What to do

1 Using a pencil and ruler, draw a square on the pizza box 1 inch (2.5 cm) from the edge.

2 Use a knife (with adult help) to cut through three sides of the square, but not the side nearest the hinge of the box.

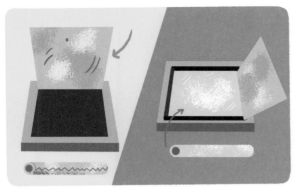

③ Open the flap and line the inside of it with foil. Stick down with white glue. Cover the square opening below the flap with cling film. Secure with electrical tape.

④ Open the box fully and line the inside of the box (bottom, sides, and lid) with foil. Glue it in place. Don't put foil over the cling film.

⑤ In the bottom of the box, add a sheet of black paper and tape in place.

⑥ Position your oven in bright sunshine. Open the lid and use a stick to prop the lid open at a 90 degree angle. Tape in place.

⑦ Make a "sandwich" of crackers, chocolate, and marshmallow and place on a piece of foil. Place this on the black paper in the solar oven. Leave in the sunshine for about half an hour, until the marshmallow has melted, then carefully remove and eat!

How does it work?

This solar oven uses several techniques to channel the power of the sun and direct it at your marshmallow:

- The aluminum foil reflects the sunlight into the oven.
- The cling film acts like a greenhouse and traps the heat inside the oven.
- The black paper acts as a "heat sink," absorbing heat from the sunlight, which helps to cook the food.

Zero-mile meal

Food can have a huge carbon footprint if it is transported from far away. A zero-mile meal on the other hand won't leave a carbon footprint at all. With your family, see how close you can get to a zero-mile meal.

Shopping for local ingredients can be a step in the right direction... ...but even better is to try growing food yourself.

Tasty tomatoes

Tomatoes are wonderful to grow in window boxes or hanging baskets; you don't even need a greenhouse. They just need good quality soil or compost, plant food, water, and sunlight to grow. Plant from February to April and harvest from July to October for best results.

Leafy bites

Lettuces can also be grown in pots by the window. They grow so quickly that you can harvest your crop just three weeks after planting! Once you cut off the tasty leaves, they'll grow again, so your plant will provide several meals.

Perhaps the easiest meal to grow at home is a salad.

Simple salad

And there you have it, a zero-mile meal! Of course, you don't have to stop at two ingredients. Use your research skills to find out how to grow other items to add to your salad, including carrots, radishes, and more.

Bedroom forest

Millions of trees are being planted around the world to reverse the effects of deforestation. You can join in by making a mini-forest on your bedroom windowsill. After all, when it comes to carbon dioxide, plants are mini trees. Better still, they're edible!

Tool kit
- empty, clean butter/ margarine tub
- paper towels or cotton wool
- water
- cress seeds

Cress is a fast-growing and delicious plant that will grow well on your windowsill.

What to do

1. Line your tub with paper towels or cotton wool and soak with water.

2. Take some cress seeds and place them into the shape of the first letter of your name...or any other simple shape.

3. Place the tub on the windowsill so that it's in sunlight. Each day, add water if the paper towels or cotton wool is dry. Don't add too much, as this could drown the seeds!

4. In about a week, the cress should have reached about 2 inches (5 cm) and will be ready to eat! With clean scissors, cut the stems of the cress about 1 inch (2 cm) from the bottom. The shoots will grow again for a second crop.

Creating compost

Kitchen and garden waste, and newspaper and cardboard can be used to make compost...just like old leaves get turned into soil with help from rainwater, earthworms, and time. This handy device can be constructed indoors, reusing a 2-liter plastic bottle.

Tool kit

- large plastic bottle
- scissors
- soil
- vegetable peelings
- newspaper and cardboard pieces
- compost maker (optional)

What to do

1 Rinse the bottle and peel off the label. Ask an adult to make a slit in the bottle. Starting from the slit, use scissors to cut around the top of the bottle. Don't cut the top off completely; leave a small hinge as shown.

2 Place 1 inch (2.5 cm) of soil in the bottom, then add 1 inch (2.5 cm) of vegetable peelings, making sure they are cut into small pieces. Add a thin layer of soil and another 1-inch (2.5-cm) layer of vegetable peelings—cover with soil.

3 Add a layer of newspaper and cardboard cut into tiny pieces and cover with soil.

4 Repeat the layers—soil, vegetable peelings, soil, vegetable peelings, soil, newspaper/cardboard—until the bottle is full almost to the cut.

5 Add a final layer of soil, and sprinkle with "compost maker" or "compost accelerator" from the garden center if you have any. (Don't worry if not; nature is good at making compost!) Sprinkle water onto the compost mix.

6 Close the bottle, seal with tape, and leave in a place with natural sunlight. It will take several months for compost to form, so be patient.

7 When compost has formed (it will look like soil and might be smelly!), you can cut the bottle about 1 inch (2 cm) above the compost.

8 Plant a seed in the compost and water it. The seed will soak up the nutrients from the compost and should grow well.

Local and global action

The environment is big and people are small. Environmental problems are often in the news, and sometimes the situation makes us feel sad and hopeless. However, there *is* hope, there *are* solutions, and people *can* make a difference.

Enjoy the environment

Get to know the environment; go to parks, forests, and the seaside. Look for animals in their natural habitats. Most of the time, the more connected people are to the environment, the happier they are. Disconnecting from TV, the Internet, phones, and other electronic devices and reconnecting with nature is highly recommended!

Small changes

Small changes can add up. If you buy locally grown fruit each week rather than imported fruit, you could be saving millions of **food-miles** per year. And every time you use a reusable shopping bag, it can prevent a plastic bag hanging around for hundreds of years.

Big changes

Governments and international organizations like the United Nations can pass laws to make environmental changes. Almost all the world's countries signed up to the Paris Agreement in 2016, which aims to limit the rise in the global average temperature.

Often it is good to think globally but act locally.

Greta Thunberg

"Ordinary" people can make extraordinary changes too. Greta Thunberg was a 15-year-old schoolchild when she first demonstrated about climate change. She held a sign outside of her country's government, acting alone. She now has millions of followers and has spoken to the United Nations and many heads of state.

SCHOOL STRIKE FOR CLIMATE

A working windmill

Nature is powerful. The sun, the wind, and flowing water can all be harnessed for power. Such renewable energy sources are far better for the environment than burning fossil fuels and releasing CO_2 into the atmosphere.

Tool kit

- large paper cup
- small paper cup
- large straw (non-plastic if possible)
- small straw
- scissors
- tape
- paper clip
- craft paper
- hole punch (or skewer)
- string

What to do

1 Turn the large paper cup upside down, then secure the large straw to it using tape. Cut so the straw is the same length as the width of the cup.

2 Trace the windmill template from p61 onto craft paper and cut out. Cut along the four solid diagonal lines and use a hole punch (or skewer) to make five holes in the places marked by gray circles.

3 Poke the small straw through the center hole. To make the sails, bend over (don't fold) the four corners with holes in. Poke the straw through each hole. Place a paperclip over the sails to hold the wheel together. Secure the back of the sails to the straw with tape. The front sails should be about ¾ inch (2 cm) in front of the back sails.

4 Poke the free end of the small straw into the big straw. Then cut the small straw so there is about 2 inches (5 cm) poking out the back of the windmill.

5 Punch two holes in the side of the small paper cup. Thread a piece of string through (like a bucket handle) and secure with knots or tape.

6 Take a second piece of string and secure one end to the bucket handle and the other to the small straw.

7 Put a small object—like an eraser, paper clip, or coin—in the bucket, then use your breath, the wind, or a hair dryer to make the windmill turn. The "wind" should cause the bucket to lift up!

Did you know?

The Persians developed the forerunner to the modern windmill over 1,000 years ago. Now there are huge "wind farms" on land and sea with hundreds of wind turbines converting wind power into electricity.

Model home

Caring for the environment starts at home. You have the chance to make improvements now... by designing and building your own **eco-friendly** model home, from recycled materials!

Decisions, decisions

Most of the activities in the book have had steps to follow, but this one is up to you. First, write a list of environmentally friendly features your home will have. Perhaps it will be powered by the sun, the wind, water. Maybe it will have a grass roof for insulation, a greenhouse, or a vertical garden included in the design, for zero-mile meals.

Building blocks

Secondly, think about materials for your model. Suggestions include plastic bottles, paper, cardboard, milk cartons, egg cartons, lollipop sticks, plastic bottle caps, aluminum foil, newspaper.

Planning on paper

Then, draw a **blueprint** of your model. Design it on paper, but don't worry if the plan changes when you get busy building it.

Making the model

Next, make your model. You may need to modify your plans as you go along, but that's okay. Keep experimenting, evaluating, and improving.

A living river

This is a story about the Whanganui River in New Zealand, which has been given the same rights as a person.

"The great River flows from the mountains to the sea. I am the River, the River is me."

This is how many Maori people of New Zealand talk of the Whanganui River. They believe that rivers and mountains are our relatives. We all live in the same space and should treat each other with respect.

For generations, the river has been a friend and provider for the locals. People built their villages along the river banks, learned how to catch 18 types of fish in sustainable quantities, and felt the river's joy, hope, and life force.

Then settlers came. They overfished. They built dams and bridges, changing the river. They dug up the riverbed for sand and rocks, diverted water for farms, factories, and a power plant, and dumped toxic waste.

The river was sad.
It spoke to the Maori,
but the settlers
didn't listen.

Things changed in 2017 when the river
was declared legally to have the same
rights as a person. Polluting or
damaging the river would be like
physically attacking a person.

A nearby, former national park, Te
Urewera, and a mountain, Taranaki,
have also been granted the rights
of a person.

The Maori and settlers are following
the principle of *kaitiakitanga*, or
guardianship, protection, and
partnership with nature.

We are the Earth,

the Earth is us.

Templates

Page 19

60

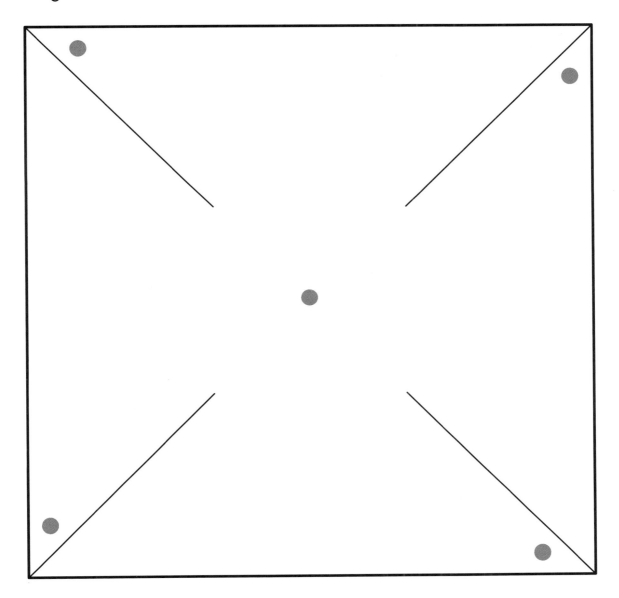

Glossary

Atmosphere The gases surrounding the Earth (or another planet, or moon)

Biodegradable Materials which can naturally be broken down (for example by bacteria), preventing pollution

Blueprint A detailed plan of something to be made, often including drawings

Carbon dioxide (CO_2) A gas formed from carbon and oxygen, which is produced when animals breathe and when fossil fuels are burned. Carbon dioxide is a greenhouse gas which can be harmful to the environment when too much is produced.

Carbon footprint The amount of carbon dioxide an activity produces

CFCs (chlorofluorocarbons) Gases made from combinations of carbon, hydrogen, chlorine, and fluorine which are harmful to the ozone layer

Climate The weather conditions in an area over a long period of time

Deforestation The act of clearing a wide area of trees

Eco-friendly Processes or materials that are friendly to the Earth and the environment, such as renewable energy and reusable materials

Endangered species Species in danger of extinction, for example through loss of habitat

Extinction When a species completely dies out

Food-miles The distance between where food is grown and where it is eaten; usually, the more food-miles, the larger the carbon footprint

Global warming An increase in the average temperature of the Earth's atmosphere due to increasing rates of greenhouse gases

Green energy Energy from renewable sources such as wind, water, and the sun's heat rather than from fossil fuels such as coal, oil and gas, or nuclear power

Greenhouse gases Gases which trap heat inside the atmosphere, much like the glass of a greenhouse prevents heat from leaving

Habitat The natural environment in which a type of plant or animal usually lives

Keystone species A species which has a large effect on the environment

Ozone layer A layer of gas in the upper atmosphere which stops harmful ultraviolet rays from reaching the Earth's surface

Plastic A type of manmade material which can be molded into almost any shape. It's non-biodegradable, so it can cause pollution, and it also has a high carbon footprint when it is produced.

Pollution When the environment is damaged by harmful substances, which could be solids, liquids, or gases

Recycling The process of converting waste materials into new objects

Reforestation The act of planting a wide area of trees; the opposite of deforestation

Sea level The average level of the sea between high tide and low tide. In recent times, the sea level has been rising due to the effects of global warming

Sustainability When a process or state can be kept at a certain level for as long as is wanted. If a new tree is planted for every tree chopped down, that is sustainable

Index

Quarto is the authority on a wide range of topics.

Quarto educates, entertains and enriches the lives of our readers—enthusiasts and lovers of hands-on living.

www.quartoknows.com

Author: Jonathan Litton
Illustrator: Pau Morgan
Consultant: Ben Ballin
Editor: Carly Madden
Designer: Mike Henson

© 2020 Quarto Publishing plc
This edition first published in 2020 by QEB Publishing, an imprint of The Quarto Group.
26391 Crown Valley Parkway, Suite 220
Mission Viejo, CA 92691, USA
T: +1 949 380 7510
F: +1 949 380 7575
www.QuartoKnows.com

All rights reserved. No part of this publication may be reproduced, stored in a retrieval system, or transmitted in any form or by any means, electronic, mechanical, photocopying, recording, or otherwise, without the prior permission of the publisher, nor be otherwise circulated in any form of binding or cover other than that in which it is published and without a similar condition being imposed on the subsequent purchaser.

A CIP record for this book is available from the Library of Congress.

ISBN 978 0 71125 052 9
9 8 7 6 5 4 3 2 1
Manufactured in Guangdong, China CC042020